I0100792

TRAIN YOUR BRAIN TO STOP OVERTHINKING

Reduce the Rhythm of Your Thoughts and Control Your Life

Ryan Cross

Copyright 2023 All rights reserved©.

The contents of this book may not be reproduced, duplicated or transmitted without the direct written permission of the author. Under no circumstances shall the publisher be held liable for any legal responsibility or liability for any repair, damage or monetary loss due to the information contained herein, either directly or indirectly.

Legal Notice:

No part of the contents of this book may be amended, distributed, sold, used, quoted or paraphrased without the author's consent.

Disclaimer Notice:

The information contained herein is for educational and entertainment purposes only. No warranties of any kind are expressed or implied. Readers acknowledge that the author is not engaged in rendering legal, financial, medical or professional advice.

INDEX

INTRODUCTION

Nowadays, modern life brings many worries and stress that generate that certain pathologies appear in our being. Within this group is the so-called *Syndrome of Accelerated Thinking* or SPA, for its acronym.

This syndrome or obsessive tendency, as it is also defined, has currently become one of the most recurrent ailments in people between 25 and 35 years of age, and not only directly affects decision-making but is also the cause of different physical ailments in generally caused by the associated psychological damage.

But what is the Accelerated Thinking Syndrome? First, you should know that there are many studies on the subject. They seek to understand what are the factors that cause this alteration and what are its main effects on the human body. We can say then that the Accelerated Thinking Syndrome is a type of compulsive behavior that has as a fundamental element the excess of information that is generated in the brain because of worries or pressures that the individual lives and other exogenous factors, which can cause an acceleration and saturation of thought to worrying levels.

Within this reality, there are many people who are not aware that they are living in this state, and believe that they are not doing themselves wrong by ruminating their thoughts, but the truth is that it is a dangerous practice with many consequences in the general welfare.

What should you do to regain control?

There are many techniques that can be applied to correct this problem with our level of thinking and through this book, we will develop them to serve as tools to know and face the problem.

The first step we must take is to realize that our thoughts are getting out of hand.

How do we realize this?

A very simple way is to analyze if more than three hypothetical scenarios are created in front of any problem in our mind. This is a direct sign that our mind is overthinking.

You need to find a way to distract yourself with your body to free your cognitive systems: go for a run, do yoga, meditation, deep breathing, or practice a sport, art or hobby that you enjoy.

Mindfulness or meditation can also help to decongest your mind, although you will need some practice and patience.

A good advice is to let the problems flow and observe them as if you were watching it rain, without developing them, because fighting against something that we cannot change at the moment, or with the tools we have, can only bring you more inconveniences than solutions.

In this book, you will find detailed techniques to calm your mind and stop overthinking.

CHAPTER 1

Causes of racing thoughts syndrome and intrusive thoughts

Causes of accelerated thinking syndrome

SPA is a type of anxiety. Too much information, too much activity, worry and social pressures can accelerate your mind to a frightening speed.

In the digital age, this is happening with an intensity never seen before.

In other words, we have irresponsibly and very seriously changed the thought-building process.

The excess of information and digital intoxication cause the memory trigger to fire a lot, and open a frightening number of windows (of the memory file), without anchoring in any, so it is normal to lose focus and concentration.

The result is a frightening and sterile speed of thoughts. Many of them useless. One of the consequences of this is that, for example, a reader reads a page of a book or newspaper and remembers nothing.

Why do I tend to think too much?

This must be a frequent question going around in your head, because the truth is that most people in today's age have a tendency to overthink. In fact,

Usually, those who have this tendency to overthink things, tend to question every decision they make and imagine different scenarios that could have happened at every moment.

'My head thinks things I don't want to think'.
Overthinking is usually related either to something from the past or to concerns about our future. In these cases, we tend to think about others, how we should do things or the reason behind some of our past decisions.

In this way, we do not focus on solving the problems; we simply start immersing ourselves in a series of thoughts that go nowhere.

Overthinking is different from self-reflection. Reflecting on different aspects of our personality or life is useful because we try to learn something about it. That is, unlike the problem of overthinking, it has a purpose.

How does one know that SPA is actually a "new" type of anxiety and not one of the already known disorders?
There are many types of anxiety: generalized anxiety disorder, panic syndrome, obsessive-compulsive disorder, *"burnout"* syndrome, and post-traumatic anxiety...

These types of anxiety arise from conflicts, develop during personality formation, personal losses, crises, abuse and untreated frustrations.

But SPA anxiety comes from stressful and hectic lifestyles and in many cases, there are no historical causes.

Due to the excess of information and activities, social networks and digital intoxication, millions of children, adolescents and adults promote the creation of thoughts and emotions in an exaggerated way without the need for trauma. And sooner or later, the syndrome of accelerated thinking causes concentration deficit.

What are the symptoms of SPA?

Lack of sleep, difficulty falling asleep, waking up tired, lumps in the throat, intestinal disorders and sometimes even increased blood pressure.

If there are headaches and muscle aches, it may be an alarm that the brain is exhausted by excessive thoughts and worries.

Psychic symptoms include suffering in anticipation of something, irritability, difficulty handling frustration, and difficulty living with people who function at a slower pace.

In addition to lack of concentration, another important and very characteristic symptom is memory deficit.

Nowadays, it is very common that children, teenagers, parents, cannot remember names of people, appointments and daily activities.

According to experts, we are accelerating the human mind at a frightening speed.

But aren't some of the symptoms the same as other types of anxiety?

Many symptoms are common to all types of anxiety, but what makes SPA different is the absence of trauma.

In addition, symptoms such as difficulty in living with slow people, excessive fatigue upon awakening, suffering in anticipation, and memory deficit are greatly exacerbated in a hyper-thinking mind or one suffering from SPA.

Types of toxic thoughts

There are many types of toxic thoughts, but some of the ones we turn to most often are the following:

Criticism: when we reproach, judge or condemn another person, we are actually vetoing ourselves. Our self-esteem is devalued and all our impotence is projected onto the other person.

Pity: victimhood is one of the obstacles that our mind puts in our way so that we cannot progress. The change is to get out of this self-sentimental pity and not to become engrossed in negative, frustrating or impotent thoughts.

Assumptions: the only job that assumptions have is to wear us down. Conjectures, guesses or figurations only damage and generate mental overweight in an almost automatic way. How can we pretend to find out what someone thinks about us, if we are often not even capable of knowing it ourselves?

Conditionals: "if I had done this, now...", "maybe I should have gone...". If you didn't do it at the time, don't torment yourself. What's done is done. Now you can only learn from it. Those thoughts only judge you and end up self-destructing you.

Why is SPA believed to be the evil of the century?

Because of the intensity and drama of this syndrome, it can affect you, as well as people of all cultures and ages.

Between 70% and 80% of human beings, including children, have manifestations of this condition. It is undoubtedly the disease of the century, more so than depression.

SPA in the digital age has already caused intense disruption and impairment in the quality of socioemotional life in all modern peoples and cultures.

How can this syndrome be prevented?

One must learn to contemplate how beautiful it is to surrender and be enraptured while observing beautiful things, such as the nature of flowers...

Talk about your failures so that your children or students understand that no one gets to the podium without having failed before.

Another tool, although much more ambitious, is to change the age of world education, to move from the age of information to the age of managing the human mind, but for that you have to challenge puzzling thoughts, criticize ideas and recycle stifling emotions.

Another very important technique is to change behavior from pointing out failures to praising and applauding the successes of your children and employees.

Remember that an expert error detector is suitable for repairing machines but not for forming brilliant and emotionally healthy minds.

What are intrusive thoughts?

Have you ever been driving down a highway, listening to the radio, when suddenly your brain says, "Hey, what if I turn onto the median that separates the highways?"?

Or maybe you grabbed a knife to cut some bread and wondered, "What if I hurt someone with this?"

These are examples of intrusive thoughts, those that pop into your head or on their own in any situation you find yourself in.

Ideally, we recognize them and then simply push them aside and move on. But for some people, dismissing intrusive thoughts can become more difficult at certain times in their lives.

From a broader perspective, an intrusive thought is anything random that "pops into the mind," explains clinical psychologist Mark Freeston, who specializes in obsessive-compulsive disorder (OCD) and anxiety disorders at Newcastle University in the United Kingdom.

An example might be a sudden panic that you left the oven on and your house is going to burn down.

This is the kind of thing we all think about from time to time. We may not think of it as 'unwanted' because it's just a thought that we quickly forget.

Then there are the intrusive thoughts that are actually unwanted, in mental health problems such as OCD, post-traumatic stress disorder (PTSD) and social anxiety.

"In social anxiety, the intrusive thoughts would probably be 'How do others see me,' 'Is my hand shaking,'" Freeston says. Whereas, in OCD, the thoughts may be contamination fears, or in PTSD, they may be flashbacks or memories of a traumatic event.

In psychology, what marks an intrusive thought as distinct from a worry or other type of thought is that it is at odds with what you generally believe to be true, or with your values. Psychologists refer to this as 'egodystonic' thinking.

Concerns are considered more "egosyntonic," meaning they are more aligned with your beliefs.

For example, if you've been reading about the rising costs of energy and basic grocery items, and you're starting to spend more than you earn, it's understandable to worry about how you'll pay your bills, but that would be a concern, not an intrusive thought.

What causes intrusive thoughts?

It is important to reiterate that intrusive thoughts are normal and often, the cause of them is simply the constant bubbling of ideas and memories in our busy brains.

According to Radomsky, sometimes there is a trigger for such thoughts: seeing a fire extinguisher, for example, and then wanting to rush home and check that the house hasn't burned down. But sometimes they are really random; just the result of our minds being "noisy."

However, what about those people whose intrusive thoughts bother them? Do their brains work differently? Perhaps they do.

Are intrusive thoughts normal?

Yes, absolutely, yes.

Adam Radomsky, lead author of a 2014 study and who works at Concordia University in Montreal, Canada, says he believes we all have intrusive thoughts.

"We know that people are more likely to notice them or struggle with them during stressful periods," he says. "But most of them, we probably don't notice them."

Intrusive thoughts are more likely to appear in times of stress.

Perhaps the fact that you have them is the result of important processes going on in your brain: if we never had random thoughts or considered things we didn't believe to be true, how would we create abstract art or dream fantastic fiction?

Freeston agrees that intrusive thoughts are "part of the human condition" and adds that it is beneficial for humans to have random thoughts all the time.

"One of the arguments that has been made is that if we didn't have random thoughts, we would never solve problems," he says.

In OCD, the relationship between intrusive thinking and creativity has been explored as a way of dealing with the condition directly.

Surprisingly, writing down random thoughts could be a way to tap into them instead of allowing them to block your brain.

When do they become a problem?

What tends to determine whether intrusive thoughts are problematic is how you respond to them.

"Someone might think of something strange and evil going on," Freeston says. "If you were Stephen King, you'd say, 'That's a great idea.' And then you write a novel."

But if you think, "what kind of person has this strange thought?" or "it could mean I'm this horrible person I think I am." From there, an intrusive thought could become an obsession."

What if my intrusive thoughts are real?

Remember that intrusive thoughts tend to be at odds with people's actual beliefs or values.

Therefore, a person with an eating disorder may have intrusive thoughts about being overweight. Someone who took a test and was happy with the result may have the sudden thought that he or she answered several questions wrong, even though he or she knew the answer.

Pandemic and intrusive thoughts

It is common to notice an increase in certain types of intrusive thoughts following specific events such as the covid pandemic.

Likewise, a person with OCD may have intrusive thoughts about something bad happening because he or she has been contaminated by germs or because certain items are not ordered a certain way. And those thoughts can still arise even if that person may know for a fact that, most likely nothing bad will happen.

Sometimes, however, real-life events occur that can confuse things, like when the pandemic broke out, for example. Disease outbreaks are known to temporarily increase intrusive thoughts about the disease suffered, and in the world, we've been living in since 2020, contamination of environments or spaces and possible contagion is a legitimate concern.

So, if you have intrusive thoughts about places contaminated with the virus or about getting covid, is that something to worry about?

Meredith Coles, director of the Binghamton Anxiety Clinic at Binghamton University, New York, reflects on this question.

"In some respects, I could argue that your anxiety should have increased in the last year or two, as you may have had more intrusive thoughts," he says, adding that a little anxiety may not be a bad thing if it motivates you to take care of yourself, eat healthier, etc. "Does that mean you have OCD?" "Or maybe it means you're human and you're going through a pandemic?"

I'm sure we've all been through a difficult time. But what about those of us who already suffer from OCD - could covid exacerbate the condition? An Italian study published in 2021 indicated that it could.

For the study, 742 people completed questionnaires. Respondents who scored high on certain questions normally used in the diagnosis of OCD tended to perceive covid as more dangerous.

However, a high health anxiety score (formerly known as hypochondriasis) was more strongly associated with coronavirus worry.

Coles believes that as we move past the peak of the pandemic, we should see any increase in intrusive thoughts recede. "We are more resilient than we sometimes think," she continues. Although he does advise doing certain things after becoming aware of our anxieties, such as seeking support from friends and family and turning off the news from time to time.

CHAPTER 2

Effects on our daily life: signs that you tend to think too much

The first step in controlling 'unhelpful' or harmful thoughts in our mind is to become aware of those signals that indicate we are thinking too much.

Sometimes people who have their brains constantly thinking about their problems tend to believe that having this habit is helpful. The reality is that research shows that thinking too much about someone or a particular problem is bad for your mental health and does nothing to prevent or solve what is bothering you so much.

Therefore, it is important to be aware of the signs of SPA:

Reliving embarrassing moments: people who have a tendency to overthink often have the habit of reliving those moments when they had a bad time.

Having trouble sleeping: a person who thinks about things a lot often experiences trouble sleeping due to anxiety or worrisome thoughts.

Trying to see the 'hidden meaning' of events: these thinking problems often arise because people try to predict the behavior of others in order to see things that may confirm their theories.

Reliving mistakes: people who tend to think about others or their problems excessively end up mentally replaying those conversations they had with people or what they could have done better.

Not being focused on solutions: the anxiety in our thoughts is usually focused on insisting over and over again on the same problem instead of being focused on finding a solution to them.

Having repetitive thoughts: you may be familiar with the expression 'my head is going to explode'. This happens to those who have the problem of repeating these thoughts over and over again.

It is difficult to make decisions: When a person has this tendency to overthink, he or she is often convinced that thinking more and analyzing a situation from different angles can help him or her make better decisions. Research on the subject tends to point to precisely the opposite. Overthinking things tends to make it more difficult to make decisions.

What are the consequences of overthinking?

Studies show that thinking too much about things can be related to experiencing too much stress and even suffering from disorders such as depression or anxiety.

Experiencing these problems of overthinking can lead to never being in the present and becoming too anchored in the past or the future.

Many people who have this tendency to overthink often end up having trouble concentrating on specific tasks.

Mental overweight

If you feel that your body is constantly tired, stiff or sore, you may be suffering from this condition.

Now, I am not referring to an increase in physical volume, nor to an increase in your cranial perimeter, but to a mental overweight. An excess of negative, inert and unproductive thoughts.

During the day, we imagine, we understand, we reflect, we create, we calculate, we make decisions... In short, we live by thinking. But not all thoughts are valid or useful, in fact, sometimes we think too much in a useless way and we produce an indigestion of useless thoughts.

If we bring up ideas that do not bring us anything nor take us anywhere, in the end, the mind ends up exhausting itself: it becomes heavy, corrodes, blocks and renounces to exercise other natural and positive processes.

We unbalance the basic unit of the mind: thoughts.

As we have seen, thinking is part of human nature. In fact, it is one of the processes that differentiate us from other living beings. However, contrary to popular belief, our thinking is not mostly conscious. Quite the contrary.

Let us think of an iceberg. The tip of the iceberg, or what is exposed on the surface, would be the conscious thought. Meanwhile, the ice that is submerged, which is the vast majority of it, constitutes the unconscious part.

According to Dr. Michael Shadlen, senior researcher at the Mortimer B. Zuckerman Behavioral Brain Institute at Columbia (USA), "the vast majority of thoughts that circulate in our brains occur in our brains," he says.

Below the radar of conscious awareness, which means that even though our brain is processing them, we are not aware when they appear or are created."

And bearing in mind that the quality of our thoughts determines our day to day life, depending on the conscious and unconscious ideas that cross our mind, so will be the result of our development.

We fill our minds with junk thoughts

Stephen Fleming, professor at University College London (UCL) conducted an interesting study in 2010. He found that people who thought more about their decisions, who overanalyzed things without reaching clear conclusions, had more cells in the prefrontal cortex.

However, what we may initially consider as something "positive" is actually not so. Because what we have is an excess of cells that do not fulfill clear functions. In fact, when comparing electroencephalograms with people with schizophrenia or autism, the same phenomenon was seen.

The conclusion they reached was the following: thinking is good, but not too much, and even less so if what we do is fall into meaningless loops.

Junk thoughts are those whose recurrence exhausts us because they do not bring us any kind of benefit. They are empty and even toxic reasonings. And they originate in our conscious mind.

In other words, mental overweight is not the result of repressed mental processes, impulses or desires but the result of deliberate elaboration. They are superfluous and unnecessary, therefore which, instead of providing us with greater self-knowledge and cognitive advantages, wear us down energetically and slow down the rest of conscious processing.

They prevent us from being creative, understanding or learning new skills. They block us and paralyze our virtues. So when we are mentally overweight, our thoughts act like junk food. And they cause physical consequences that can even be analogous to those of obesity. Among them, physical exhaustion, which causes difficulty in walking or physical exertion. Also, problems in breathing normally, increased sweating, generalized pain in the joints or even skin alterations such as acne, flaking or skin irritations.

Overthinking

Overthinking is a term that refers to the tendency to dwell obsessively, to incessantly repeat thought patterns that lead to a vicious cycle of worry, anxiety, nervousness and self-doubt.

Why does it occur?

The person prone to *overthinking* spends a good part of his or her free time -even busy time- thinking things over. Generally, this unhealthy habit is more frequent when it comes to solving "everyday" problems: work, family, couples, friendships, etc.

This tendency to ruminative thinking is very common, especially when it comes to remembering past events or imagining future ones. In the first case, some people are capable of spending days and days analyzing a past conversation down to the smallest detail: they study gestures and words as if there were a way to go back in time to turn that conversation into something "perfect".

Likewise, there is also a tendency to *overthink* future events, preparing, for example, all the details of a more or less relevant work meeting obsessively, even the physical position to be adopted in the chair.

It is like a kind of torture where the past is relived over and over again and the future is imagined repeatedly.
If constant noise about the past and the most inconsequential future occupies a good part of your thinking, you are abusing *overthinking*, and this is mainly due to fear and perfectionism.

Fear of failure, of things going wrong and, as a consequence, tormenting ourselves afterwards. And the erroneous -and dangerous- belief that we are capable of reaching perfection in our actions and behavior. As if one day, far in the future, we will be able to sit satisfied on a sofa saying: "I've finally made it, I'm perfect".

Likewise, fear of failure grips and scrambles our thinking, incapacitating our ability to transform reflection into action.

Perfectionism, on the other hand, can hide high doses of self-centeredness but also insecurity and victimhood. As we have a high regard for our potential capabilities but will never be able to fully achieve them, we will always remain immersed in a vicious circle of frustrations, regrets and curses.

The dangers of *overthinking*

Having a lot of repetitive thoughts can be one of the most dangerous things there is. Why should you stop thinking the same thing over and over again?

Does *overthinking* keep you from making a single decision or concentrating on what you need to do?

The act of "overthinking or overthinking" may be associated with psychological problems such as anxiety or depression, although experts find it difficult to know which comes first.

Amy Morin, psychotherapist and regular contributor to Forbes Inc. in an article for this platform on the 10 signs of overthinking, states that this condition involves continually reliving the past and worrying excessively about the future. In addition, she says that there can be 2 types of "*overthinking*":

One that is different from "healthy problem solving". When you are in a difficult situation, it results in a healthy problem-solving process only when it is necessary. Overthinking on the other hand, in this case, involves dwelling on that problem over and over again.

Other than "self-reflection". Self-reflection involves learning and gaining a perspective of oneself regarding a defined situation and is purposeful. Overthinking, in this case, is instead delving into what you have no control over and then thinking about how bad this makes you feel, so you can't develop a clear picture of the situation.

In itself, overthinking is like listening to your mind spinning endlessly without getting anywhere, nor doing so from a healthy and positive perspective. You may not understand its literal meaning, but if you have experienced it, you probably know what I mean.

What are the physical and mental dangers of overthinking?

Everything has consequences, even turning your thoughts over a thousand times.

It can increase stress. As your sense of clarity and your ability to solve problems are impaired, this can increase feelings of stress and lead you to experience mental health problems.

It can trigger anxiety and depression. Feelings of worry intensify and fear, sadness and hopelessness set in. Also, it can manifest with anger or irritability that eventually cause depression and you will have a higher risk of experiencing addiction.

It affects the immune system response. Stressful situations cause hormones or substances such as cortisol to be produced unnecessarily, which can be detrimental to your immune system and cause different imbalances.

It can make you lose your creativity. When everything is calm in your brain and in your head, all cognitive and creative processes develop and happen more easily and naturally.

While overthinking can generate new and fresh ideas, it can also be counterproductive and create mental roadblocks that make it challenging to think outside the box.

Another study published in the journal Scientific Reports found that when certain parts of the brain and cognitive processes are calm, we are more creative.

It can increase your blood pressure and the risk of cardiovascular disease. As a result of stress, it can increase your blood pressure and aggravate factors that increase the risk of heart disease, such as smoking, increased cholesterol levels, unhealthy diet, etc.

It alters your sleep. When you feel that your brain is not disconnected, your sleep pattern and the quality of your sleep will be altered. You will find it difficult to fall asleep and, therefore, you will have an unrefreshing sleep.

The body needs to enter a calm state in order to sleep: the heart rate should slow down, as should blood pressure and breathing.

Over-analyzing can be exciting, especially when thoughts are racing and this can take us out of the calm state the body needs to sleep.

You may have changes at the digestive level. When you are stressed or thinking over and over again, digestive discomfort may appear and eventually cause irritable bowel syndrome, gastritis or even ulcers in the digestive tract.

It affects your memory. Overthinking obviously puts unnecessary work on your brain and this affects your cognitive ability and can hinder your memory.

Change your appetite. Stress can suppress or exaggerate your appetite by secreting certain hormones that affect your usual food intake.

Specialists argue that people do it to distract themselves or even to calm down.

It can paralyze you. In a manner of speaking, it can encourage non-action, as you will feel unable to make decisions, to solve problems and, therefore, to take action and undertake.

This is called "paralysis by analysis", a concept that consists of thinking about possible consequences that may occur, or simply worrying about certain results that may not be to our liking.

Here's what happens to the body when you think too much

Replaying past conversations, mulling over choices, or getting caught in a tunnel of "what if" scenarios are some of the symptoms of overthinking.

The excess of information saturates the cerebral cortex, producing a hyper-thinking, agitated, low tolerance, impatient and uncreative mind.

Information overload, the demands of multi-tasking and the accumulation of worries have dire consequences on physical and psychological well-being and can accelerate the mind at a frightening speed. In the digital age, this is happening with an intensity never seen before.

One study found that 73% of adults between the ages of 25 and 35 think too much, as do 52% of people aged 45 to 55.

Interestingly, research has found that many overthinkers believe they are actually doing themselves a favor by repeating their thoughts. But the truth of the matter is that, as you've already found, overthinking is a dangerous game that can have many negative consequences for our well-being.

"Thinking is good; thinking with a critical conscience is even better, but thinking in excess is a bomb against the quality of life," said the renowned psychiatrist, researcher and writer Augusto Cury.

Does all this sound familiar?

Intense acceleration of thought construction predisposes, among other things, to chronic dissatisfaction, delayed emotional maturity, emotional distress and the development of psychiatric disorders, and psychosomatic illnesses, compromises creativity and overall intellectual performance, impairs social relationships and hinders the ability to work in a team and cooperate socially.

The emotional, intellectual, social and physical consequences of accelerated thinking are enormous. And while they may not always manifest themselves in the present, they will certainly appear in the future.

"In this stressful, fast-paced and hectic society, it is not easy to resolve this issue completely. But, if it is not possible to eliminate it, human beings need and must manage it and to do so, it is vital to be as free as possible to think without being a slave of thoughts. Being able to avoid the suffering of anticipation and to purify the mind through the DCD (doubt, criticize and determine) technique is key."

Among the most important points to prevent this state learning to manage intrusive thoughts when they appear is one of the main ones. "One cannot let the mind think what it wants when it wants, nor suffer or worry in advance. The mind is a vehicle and unfortunately, the vast majority of human beings have not learned anything about how to manage thoughts," concluded Cury.

When thinking "too much" is positive

To complete our understanding of the concept of *overthinking,* we must differentiate this kind of musing from more serene reflection.

Overthinking is especially negative when it appears linked to everyday events, small problems and daily setbacks to which we commonly devote more time than they deserve: a family argument, a bad day at work, an unrewarding conversation on Whatsapp or even the defeat of your favorite team.

If we do a simple mathematical operation of the amount of time we spend thinking about all those daily events, we will realize that they occupy a good part of our mind throughout the day, exhausting, in many cases, our mental energy reservoir, to the point of not having time or strength for "other" kind of thinking.

And those other kinds of reflections are the ones that occur when the mind is in "serene mode" and the "big" ideas emerge, the ones that go a little further than a meeting or the scratch on your brand new car.

After all, the world advances thanks to the fact that we are capable of thinking "too much" about the great human questions, without forgetting, in this sense, that doubt - not the doubt of which shirt to wear to dazzle at the presentation, whether the pink or the blue one - is the basis of science, philosophy and the engine of knowledge.

The French philosopher Peter Abelard, inspired by Aristotle, said: "The principle of wisdom is found in doubt; by doubting we arrive at the question and by seeking the answer we can arrive at the truth".

CHAPTER 3

Break the cycle: techniques for controlling overthinking

Trapped by your own thoughts?

You stare at the ceiling of your room, wishing you could go to sleep. Thoughts race through your head, holding your mind hostage. Or you reflect on the awkward conversation you had with your boss on the way home from work.

Overthinking can happen at any time of the day or night and can leave people frozen in indecision.

People are often trapped by their own thoughts because they are striving for perfection or trying to find a way to control a situation, said Kimber Shelton, a psychologist and owner of KLS Counseling & Consulting Services in Duncanville, Texas.

"We want to figure out all the angles and be able to control what would happen if this were to happen, and we get stuck in this process of overthinking," he points out.
Shelton said that when people think too much, their thoughts start to spin and they can't find a conclusion.

Thoughts of mishandled or embarrassing past events can also disturb people and lead them to replay the events in their head over and over again, he added.

"Overthinkers have trouble prioritizing their problems and understanding which problems are or are not under their control," said Deborah Serani, a psychologist and associate professor at the Gordon F. Derner Institute for Advanced Psychological Studies at Adelphi University in Garden City, New York.

How to break the cycle of overthinking?

Serani created a five-step process to escape the endless cycle of overthinking.

Step 1: The first step is to be aware when you are thinking too much. Sometimes other people will point this out to you, and while it can be irritating to hear, it is helpful to learn to detect it within yourself.

In his case, Serani said his palms get sweaty and his heart starts beating faster when he thinks too much.

Step 2: The next step is to look back and get a perspective on what you're overthinking and whether you have any control over it. "Am I thinking about something that is beyond my control, or is it something I can control?" expresses Serani.

You may not be able to control the traffic, but you may be able to control the route you take next time, the GPS you use to get around traffic jams, the drink in your cup holder, and how you react to the situation.

If it's something you can't control, you can say to yourself, "I have to really prioritize what I have the ability to change," and traffic is something I can't change, the psychologist points out.

Step 3: If the situation is under your control, the third step is to be in the moment and isolate the singular problem. Breathe deeply and slowly three times, inhaling through your nose and exhaling through your mouth. Concentrate on the sensation of the air going in and out. Write down your problem on a sheet of paper and possible solutions. Make a decision or postpone it for another time when your mind is clearer.

Step 4: Once you have identified a problem, the next step is to set a time limit on how much time you will devote to solving the problem.

It is important not to keep going over and over the problem, as it is not effective in solving the problem at hand, says Serani.

For example, if you are stuck in traffic and are going to be late for an appointment, you can become a problem solver and look for alternative routes, call the person you are meeting to let them know you will be late, or take a deep breath while listening to the radio.

The teacher explains that someone who is left pondering the problem might think, "I can't believe I'm stuck in traffic" or "I'm going to be late for this appointment; that makes me look really bad professionally."

Step 5: The final step is to acknowledge the small steps you took to solve your problem, even if you couldn't solve it completely. "You're going to celebrate the fact that you took a situation, acknowledged that you were overthinking, and tried to solve the problem."

Many people may not be successful the first couple of times they practice this method, and she emphasized that it is normal to feel this way.

How to stop thinking about something?

There are a number of strategies that allow you to stop thinking about certain problems, ideas, or people. Among them, we can find the following tips on how to relax your mind and not think about anything, so take note:

Get out of your head: sometimes, we don't realize that we are too immersed in our thoughts. Therefore, in order to know how to control the thoughts that keep you absorbed, it is important that you try to 'get out' of your head.

To do this, we can resort to distracting ourselves with activities that we like, this can be painting, dancing, singing, knitting, taking care of your plants or your garden, exercising, writing, learning a language, in short, anything that you like and distracts you positively.

Reason for your thoughts: these thinking problems are usually due to irrational beliefs about ourselves or others. Thus, it is highly advisable to try to control these thoughts by reasoning with them.

Learn to live in the present: focusing your attention on what you are doing will help you stop thinking about someone or certain problems. Meditation or *mindfulness* are two practices that will help you achieve this habit.

Write down your thoughts: instead of keeping thoughts in your head, write them down in a journal. This makes us give less weight to those thoughts and helps us to stop thinking about it.

"Saturation **of thought"**: by saturation, we often achieve a paradoxical effect: by recreating and concentrating on thinking and rethinking without limit what we want to avoid thinking, what we will do is saturate ourselves and then during the day that thought may not come back to us with such intensity.

Go to therapy: overthinking, especially when it is in excess, may be associated in certain cases with some mental health problems. Therefore, if this anxiety of excessive thoughts is hindering you from being happy, it may be necessary to turn to a professional psychologist.

How to stop *overthinking?*

Stopping this storm of obsessive ideas that go round and round in your head is not a simple process. It is not as easy as hitting the *off* button to "turn off" our brain, but there are different more or less practical options that can help you put a stop to the excess of recurring thoughts.

Redirect your thinking

We cannot turn off the mind, our brain is in a constant boiling of ideas. But we can redirect those thoughts to less harmful areas and constructive actions. To begin with, we must learn to relax and disconnect.

It is not bad to look for different solutions to a problem, but if we cannot "find the key" after a reasonable time, it is better to leave it at least until further notice. Even in some situations, if we are not able to find the solution in a reasonable time, maybe doing nothing about it is just the "solution".

In this sense, we must remember that it is useless to try to control everything and intervene in every situation to prove our worth and capacity. On the contrary, giving in and delegating is an act of modesty and practical intelligence.

Likewise, another way to redirect your thinking is to radically change your mind. If you can't deal with one thing that worries you, deal with something else. You'll see how soon the first situation doesn't seem so worrisome.

After all, redirecting the mind involves controlling the thought instead of it controlling you. Because, as we said, we are not able to stop thinking... or are we?

Meditate
There are many different meditation techniques that help to unravel the confusion of thought and the usual boiling of ideas. With just a few minutes a day, meditation can give you the mental energy to recharge your need to face any challenge.

The advocates of this formula define meditation as a kind of mental exercise comparable to the one we practice with our physical body. But as with any exercise, you also need a learning period.

Meditation is not exactly about leaving the "mind blank", but to manage the thought, managing precisely those obsessive thoughts until we distance ourselves from them enough to visualize their essence and solve them in a simple way.

Thus, for example, the transcendental meditation of the famous Maharishi Mahesh Yogi -or of the filmmaker David Lynch- seeks a state of full consciousness but free of any mental control. Analyzed from a scientific point of view in various studies, it is considered an activity that can reduce stress and increase psychological flexibility.

On the internet, there are many examples of guided meditation; you can search and select the one you like the most, you can also look for a school or a trained instructor.

Relativizes past and future
You know what they say: if you live with one foot in the past and one in the future, your present passes you by.

Living in the present is a mantra that has haunted us since the beginning of time; so simple to understand and so complicated to apply.

But living in the present does not mean forgetting the past and denying the future; that would be impossible as well as irresponsible. We all have a past and a future that underpin our identity. But we should not fall into the trap of living with our backs to the present, something very common in people with a tendency to *overthink*.

If you spend a good part of your time mentally solving the past and taking out your umbrella for the torments of the future, you miss the beauty of the moment.

How long has it been since you've taken a close look at that tree in front of your house, or that bird chirping outside your window every morning? Too busy figuring out your (small) world?

Don't worry, your world will keep spinning, even if you take a little time to enjoy the present. More importantly, your mind and body will thank you for it.

Sleep hygiene: 8 ways to train your brain for better sleep

Relaxing in the evening

Overthinking affects many people at night as they toss and turn in bed.

If incessant thoughts are keeping you awake, Shelton recommends scheduling time to overthink. "I'll give myself five minutes and allow my brain to go wherever it needs to go," he said. After you've done those five minutes, move on to another task.

Engage in some relaxing self-care activities, such as bathing, meditating or listening to music.

Another strategy is to write down your worries to allow your thoughts to escape your brain. They can be written down as you think about them, or you can create a list of pros and cons of what you are thinking about.

Deep breaths

It's a fact. The act of breathing slowly, comfortably and deeply slows down the heartbeat and tells our nervous system to relax. Take ten deep breaths inhaling through your nose, holding the air inside you for 5 to 10 seconds and exhaling through your mouth as slowly as you can without forcing yourself or feeling uncomfortable or dizzy.

Meditate

I say it and I repeat it again throughout the book: meditate. Whether or not you believe it is for you, believe me: it is for you. Meditate if you find yourself overwhelmed if you have anxiety or feel stress. Meditate even if you've had a great day. We are not talking here about spiritual matters but about scientific evidence. Closing your eyes to relaxing music with no background lyrics and breathing quietly isolates you from everything else. It reminds your mind that it can slow down from time to time. And it certainly allows you to escape from your responsibilities for a few moments. And that's magical, healthy and much needed. Allow yourself to disconnect for 6 minutes a day. And maybe you say to me, "but I don't have time". Aren't you reading this book right now? Don't you have five minutes a day to take care of your mental health? I'm sure you do. Give yourself a mental vacation and meditate today. I assure you that only good things can happen to you when you practice meditation.

Try not to think too much while meditating

Meditation is a common self-care practice that focuses on having a mind free of thoughts. For an over-thinker, this can be especially difficult.

When you find that your mind wanders during meditation, that is, when a thought suddenly appears, simply let it pass, do not develop it and refocus your mind on your breath.

The point is not not to think. The point is not to develop those thoughts that arise spontaneously and to focus your attention on your breathing again. You will gain precious seconds of silence and calm until your next thought. And those moments are pure gold for your mental health and well-being.

If you are a beginner, start with 30 seconds of meditation and then slowly build up to longer times.

Meditation is not something that everyone can do easily at first. Like everything else it needs practice and patience, so don't think you are failing if you can't do it.

Practice exercise

Yes, I know, you've heard it many times. But exercising is one of the most powerful antidepressants and mental relaxants there is. Not only will you have countless huge benefits on a physical level, but also on a mental level. It will make you feel calmer throughout the day, more positive, more focused and upbeat, and it will help you fall asleep easily.

Spend at least thirty minutes 3 to 5 times a week practicing any sport or moderate exercise. If you don't have equipment, walk fast. Go for a swim, play paddle tennis with your partner. Do some push-ups and squats or, if you feel motivated,

some tables that you find on the internet of high-intensity exercises, tabata, calisthenics or crossfit. It will be 15-20 minutes of exercise and you will work every muscle in your body. And not only will you feel great, but you will also start to look better physically.

Watch your diet at night

Heavy or unhealthy eating will worsen our quality of sleep and also make it more difficult for us to fall asleep easily.

Avoid consuming excessive amounts of food, fried foods or sweets before going to bed and, if possible, eat dinner three to four hours before going to sleep. This will make your body lighter and you will not have problems when resting properly.

Drink relaxing infusions

Any infusion will do, as long as it is hot. Drinking a hot liquid at night regulates our blood pressure and prepares us for our well-deserved rest.

The best relaxing herbal teas are lemon balm, valerian, chamomile, passionflower, lavender, lemon verbena and lime blossom.

Seek professional help

If you find yourself thinking too much for weeks or months, it may be time to seek professional help. You could end up with a mental disorder, such as generalized anxiety.

"Generalized anxiety is a very common experience, particularly since covid started because there is a lot of pressure with the pandemic and life changes," states Serani. Overthinking can also be triggered by past trauma, Shelton adds.

Therapy can help heal that trauma so that "our thoughts are no longer dictated by a past event and we can create thoughts that are more grounded in current reality."

The most important thing: how to leave mental overweight behind and keep our mind healthy again?

We must not allow our thoughts to dominate us to avoid being besieged by mental toxicity.

That is, it is necessary to learn to control them. And for this, you can put into practice the following tips:

Rest your mind: artistic practices such as painting can help you release tension and replace junk thoughts with more productive ones. Reading, going to the movies or attending workshops and seminars can also give us a mental rest.

Eliminate social toxins: identify the social relationships that may be harming you. If you surround yourself with overly critical people, you will end up doing the same. Look for a more enriching environment that transmits strength, energy and positivity.

Stop thinking: put a stop to that toxic recurrence. Paradoxical as it may seem, concentrate as much as possible on those negative ideas. And after a few minutes dedicated entirely to them, cut them radically and abruptly. Empty your mind.

If we have negative thoughts from time to time, their physical impact will be practically negligible. But if they are constantly present, they can inhibit our capabilities and diminish our quality of life.

People who are mentally overweight seek to remove themselves from their own reality. They are individuals who need to unload their unproductive thoughts and free themselves from all the unpleasant emotions they produce. Let us not let them contaminate us.

If we take care of the quality of our thoughts, we will be taking care of the quality of our life. Let's not forget it. Remember some techniques to overcome excessive thinking:

How to stop it?
- It distracts and occupies the mind.
- Create awareness of the present moment.
- Exercise.
- Meditate or do exercises that promote deep breathing.
- Focus on finding a solution instead of focusing on the problem.
- Disconnect and establish moments with defined time for reflection.
- Explore new ways to feel good, such as providing service or volunteering.
- Recognize negative thoughts and work on transforming them into positive ones.
- Eat consciously, healthily and proportionately.
- Go out and do outdoor activities.
- Write down your thoughts on a piece of paper and read them again. In this way, you will reduce their importance and you will be able to observe them more objectively.

CHAPTER 4

Rumination and anxiety: causes, consequences, how to improve them and test

What is rumination?

Rumination is a cognitive process, which has received a great deal of empirical (evidence-based) confirmation in clinical research and is considered a factor involved in various emotional disorders: depression, anxiety, eating disorders, substance abuse, impulse dyscontrol, anger, among others, and interferes with effective problem-solving.

Rumination has been considered a style of response to discomfort, characterized by long chains of repetitive, cyclical, self-focused thoughts, such as:

- Why did I react this way?
- Why can't I concentrate?
- Why am I so tired?
- Why don't I feel good about anything?
- Why do I get depressed and others don't?
- "If I don't feel better, I won't be able to finish this task and I'll be fired," and similar thoughts that increase discomfort and lead to passive and recurrent reflection, which does not lead to active problem-solving.

Several studies have identified that it is the "cavillative" and passive component that is the most maladaptive and harmful.

Passive pondering contributes to the increase of automatic negative thoughts consistent with the state of mind, which at the same time increase the threats and possible negative consequences, constituting unproductive circles of thought that favor pessimistic and fatalistic explanations.

In short, we enter the loop: we think bad then we feel bad, ergo, we think bad and repeat the whole cycle over and over again.

On the other hand, this self-focus and recurrent thinking interferes with attentional resources, making it difficult to concentrate, increasing the probability of errors in effective problem solving, which in turn contributes to feelings of helplessness and inability to control situations and circumstances.

Rumination and worry are two closely related cognitive processes that share certain characteristics and consequences, although they can be distinguished mainly by their temporal orientation. While rumination is focused on present or past events, worry is oriented towards potential future threats.

Distinguishing them is important as it will help us to identify and choose the best strategy to deal with the situation.

How to get out of the rumination loop?
Adopt a proactive attitude, get out of the obsessive thinking or passive reflection on the problems or your current situation, recover contact with other perspectives of your current reality: laugh, talk, write, sing, cry, dance, listen to music, tidy the house, cook, meditate, read, breathe deeply... there are many solutions.

Identify what is the main fear or source of discomfort that is triggering your repetitive or obsessive thoughts. Is it related to something in the past, present or future? And most importantly, in my opinion, is there anything you can do to change the situation?

a) If the answer is yes, orient yourself towards possible solutions. In this case, although it may seem paradoxical to wonder about what is the worst that can happen, it sometimes helps to put the most likely reality into perspective and manage the consequences. Consider mistakes as opportunities for learning and personal growth. There is no single, infallible way to cope with discomfort. Creativity and flexibility are key to developing your potential.

And remember that we all make mistakes. Moreover, all those who have succeeded in history, accumulated, before succeeding, more mistakes than the rest of the people who did not succeed so much.

b) Otherwise, be ready to let go of what does not depend on you and focus on what does depend on you: how to cope better. Set concrete goals that contribute to improve your mood. Here, distraction and rewarding activities will help you focus on the present and gradually increase your sense of self-control and orientation.

Going for a walk, a hike or practicing physical exercise will help you change the course of your thoughts, allowing a new approach to the situation.

Talk to a friend. Putting words to your ruminative thoughts allows you to organize ideas and structure a coherent discourse allowing a more realistic view of things.

Write down your thoughts on paper or on the computer. It allows you to organize and structure thoughts and to clarify the motives or functions that are fulfilling obsessive thinking, ruminative thoughts or passive reflection.

Differences between reflective thinking and rumination

How many times have we found ourselves in the following situation: We have a problem or discomfort about which we think and reflect, but far from obtaining clarity and calm, or approaching a solution, we get involved and trapped in a loop of thoughts that only manages to increase our confusion and discomfort. This is obsessive thinking.

I am referring to that moment in which reflective thinking is transformed into rumination or obsessive thinking, that instant in which thoughts cease to be a way out and become the labyrinth itself.

Haven't we always been told to think twice about things?

There are situations or times with many demands, both internal and external, that increase habitual stress responses - anxiety, anger, nervousness, sadness...- and that are usually accompanied by thoughts that repeat themselves and seem to take control of our mind, contributing to great confusion, mental fatigue and physical and emotional tiredness.

At these times, doubts arise about the benefit of "thinking things through" or reflecting on our problems or emotions, as it does not seem to contribute at all to resolving situations or diminishing discomfort.

However... isn't reflective thinking one of the keys to finding effective solutions to problems, learning from our mistakes and changing our emotions?

All emotions, especially unpleasant ones, are part of our equipment for survival and allow us to cope and reorient our behavior to restore balance and well-being.

Thoughts, memory and attention are part of cognitive processes closely linked to emotions and experiential learning. They allow us to elaborate, filter and interpret external and internal reality, significantly influencing emotional experiences.

However, sometimes we tend to believe that our thoughts are real facts and that is when it becomes necessary to reflect on how we are thinking about our reality.

It is often a tendency, something characteristic of our way of coping with problems, to act in a "roundabout" way. For example, after having made a mistake, unpleasant or uncomfortable feelings such as shame, guilt, sadness, anger or anxiety arise.

Often, patients come for psychological consultation expressing difficulties in managing their thoughts: "I can't stop thinking about things". "I think I'm going to go crazy if I don't stop thinking and thinking about everything" and they expect help to stop thinking or to stop thinking.

The truth is that when repetitive or recurring thoughts invade the mind, they can become the problem themselves, increasing the discomfort that originally motivated them. But, above all, it becomes difficult to implement effective solutions to problems.

It is not a matter of suppressing thinking about our emotions, nor of ceasing to express what we feel, since that also has maladaptive consequences on our emotional management.

The dichotomy is not: to think or not to think about our problems. The central issue is the way we think.

The questions we should ask ourselves are: why, what for, what do we hope to achieve by thinking about the problem or discomfort?

This will give us clues to implement more adaptive, productive or beneficial alternatives.

Which professional can help me?

The diagnosis of Accelerated Thinking Syndrome is made by the psychologist and/or psychiatrist by performing a specific medical examination and listening to the symptoms reported by the patient and his or her history.

The symptoms are various but can be easily identified:
- Anxiety.
- Difficulty concentrating.
- Lapses of memory loss.
- Fatigue.
- Insomnia
- Irritability.
- Unrest.
- Intolerance to contrariness.
- Change of mood.
- Constant dissatisfaction.

Psychosomatic symptoms:
- Headache.
- Muscle aches and pains.
- Hair loss.
- Gastritis.

What is the treatment like?

The treatment consists of combining psychotherapy, which helps in the management of emotions and the control of thoughts and the adaptation of good life habits, such as:

- Regular physical activity.
- Moments of relaxation and leisure.
- Avoid long working days.
- Disconnect from the phone and social networks.
- Pleasant encounters with friends.
- Take care of what is really important at any given moment.
- Stop watching the news to avoid negative influences of news that can cause you stress, fear, anger, etc.
- Reduce the accelerated pace of your schedule.
- Relax.
- Organize and adapt.

It is very important to organize your life, your mind to take care of what really matters. One must learn to silence the mind, practicing meditation, mindfulness, yoga and other physical activities.

Train your mind for contemplation and get in touch with nature. Protect your emotions, laugh and smile.

Care with food and body is essential. It is also important to control access to technology and information, avoiding excesses.

The anxiety test

How do you know if you have anxiety?

In the following test, you will be able to evaluate yourself with respect to anxiety.

At the end, you will see the results according to the majority of your answers and the points obtained.

Remember that this is a guideline and is not a substitute for an evaluation by a professional.

How often do you have each symptom? Select the options that best fit you, from "never" to "almost every day".

1. Feeling overwhelmed, distressed
Never
On some occasions
Often
Almost every day

2. Feeling of uneasiness, nervousness, restlessness
Never
On some occasions
Often
Almost every day

3. Racing heart or palpitations (without any illnesses that justify it)
Never
On some occasions
Often
Almost every day

4. Feeling of fatigue
Never
On some occasions
Often
Almost every day

5. Trouble resting and sleeping (you take a long time to sleep, you wake up often, you have nightmares...).
Never
On some occasions
Often
Almost every day

6. Muscle tension or pain in some parts of the body (such as neck, back, jaw, or extremities).
Never
On some occasions
Often
Almost every day

7. Chest tightness, choking or shortness of breath
Never
On some occasions
Often
Almost every day

8. Stomach ache, nausea or vomiting
Never
On some occasions
Often
Almost every day

9. Concentration problems (even in simple tasks).
Never
On some occasions
Often
Almost every day

10. Inability to think clearly or mental block
Never

On some occasions
Often
Almost every day

11. Anticipatory, negative or catastrophic thoughts.
Never
On some occasions
Often
Almost every day

12. Lack of memory, you have trouble remembering things
Never
On some occasions
Often
Almost every day

13. Insecurity when making decisions (even simple ones).
Never
On some occasions
Often
Almost every day

14. Ruminative thoughts (you think about things a lot).
Never
On some occasions
Often
Almost every day

15. Smoking or drinking more than usual
Never
On some occasions
Often
Almost every day

16. Avoid certain situations
Never
On some occasions
Often
Almost every day

17. Changes in appetite
Never
On some occasions
Often
Almost every day

18. Changes in sexual behavior
Never
On some occasions
Often
Almost every day

19. Crying more than usual
Never
On some occasions
Often
Almost every day

20. Mood swings, irritability
Never
On some occasions
Often
Almost every day

If you have selected in more than ten answers the options "often" or "almost every day", then you are probably overthinking. If you identify yourself and if you also see that you have these or other anxiety symptoms, then you are probably suffering from anxiety. But don't worry, the first step to solve something is to recognize its existence, so you are already one step closer to solving it.

Such a test can never empirically assess generalized anxiety disorder (GAD) or any specific psychopathology (such as depression or obsessive-compulsive disorder).

It is simply a very basic self-assessment test, which serves to give you, in an orientative way, an idea of what level of anxiety you are at.

It can be helpful for you, or to start asking yourself how to help someone with anxiety.

But this self-diagnosis will never replace the judgment of a professional who has evaluated you.

Is it a test just to find out if you have anxiety or depression?

That's something we can't tell you from a 20-question test score. Mental health is more complex. Both anxiety and depression are complicated and the hard part is knowing where it comes from and why it occurred in the first place.

Finding out what causes anxiety and what we can do about it

To do so, you can turn to a professional. In this case, a psychologist.

In psychological therapy, you will discover that anxiety is overcome little by little, seeing things like:
- What causes this anxiety or sense of distress.
- How it has affected you so far.
- Irrational beliefs you have.
- How to prevent it.
- Tools and techniques to calm anxiety when it appears.

In effect: I feel excessive worry, anxiety, the desire to cry...

First of all. It is important to emphasize: feeling anxious is normal.

Many times we do not accept this emotion, or even blame ourselves for having it, which can make the symptoms even worse. However, don't you ever wonder if you shouldn't feel happy? It is the same with anxiety: it is a necessary, adaptive reaction (it fulfills a function).

It is usually a temporary and temporary feeling, but it becomes a problem when we get stuck in it.

Emotions are there to warn us, to alert us that something is happening: anxiety about a change of job, an unexpected event, an accident, an exam, financial problems...

As we said, the problem is when this anxiety becomes unmanageable: choking sensation, pressure in the chest, trembling, inability to think, fatigue, stress, intestinal problems, catastrophic thoughts, not being able to act, psychosomatic diseases, frequent sleeping problems...

If it is also intense, frequent and long-lasting, this is a dangerous combo that can lead to a spiral of discomfort.

What do I do then?

I would like to tell you not to worry, that it will pass by itself, that I'm sure it's nonsense... But no.

It's totally legitimate to feel anxiety or fear about something. I'm sure it's important and what they say about it passing on its own... well, it happens sometimes, other times things get worse if you don't pay proper attention to them. I know this from my own experience.

Every day I see people who feel anxiety. People like you and me, whose lives have been plagued by a difficulty that is difficult for them to solve.

It is so complicated for them that they are short of breath, it prevents them from sleeping. And if they could avoid it at all costs, they would. But they can't and they have to face it.

How to stop thinking so much? Here are some tips

It is clear that the human mind does not have a switch that can turn it off as we would do with a television, nor is it possible to decide which thought to watch as one who decides to watch his favorite channel on the set.

However, it is possible to make worrisome thoughts fade away, especially if you stop paying attention to them.

Let's look at some useful strategies for this:

1. Do not try to stop thinking
Although it may seem counterintuitive, one of the best things you can do to try to stop thinking so much is simply not to become obsessed with stopping intrusive thinking.

That is, if the recurring thought appears suddenly, trying to consciously stop thinking about it will only make it more vivid. Remember the techniques we talked about earlier to focus your attention on your breathing and gain the upper hand on unconscious and repetitive thoughts.

The thought will eventually disappear at some point or another, so the best thing to do is to try to ignore it and not develop it so that it passes by.

2. Do not give it importance
We are sitting quietly in our living room and suddenly, we think of the uncertainty generated by not knowing how the current political situation is going to end.

We got up from our armchairs and began to think of possible scenarios, each one more catastrophic than the last, going so far as to think that a civil war could even start.

This is an example of what not to do. If the thought comes, it should not be given more force than one who adds fuel to the fire.

The problem with ruminating is that it is something that can become addictive. If you have not been able to find an answer to the thought that generates anxiety, perhaps the best thing to do is to forget that such a solution exists.

3. Living in the moment

This may sound like cheap and utopian advice, but it is something
plausible and effective. If we focus on what we are doing at the moment, however simple it may be, we will find that it is a very good way to cut obsessive thinking.

Whether it's while doing the dishes, reading a book, or simply standing in line at the butcher's, being mindful of what you're doing and where you are takes the focus away from intrusive thinking.

It is not possible to be fully aware of two activities at the same time. For that reason, living in the moment is a very good option to take the weight off what has happened or what may happen.

4. Do not react emotionally

This may be a little more complicated, but ideally, you should remain calm when an obsessive thought occurs.

If you react, either by getting angry or sad, you enter a loop in which you look for more reasons to be worried and on top of that, you attach more gravity to the thought.

The goal is to stop paying attention to him and that also implies not giving him the pleasure of making any emotional impression on us.

5. Listen to relaxing music

This is a simple, yet convenient and economical option, especially if the songs do not have lyrics or are sung in a language you do not understand.

Although it is a somewhat far-fetched situation, it is possible that, when listening to a song sung in the native language, if something is mentioned that is related to worry, the person will go into a loop about that intrusive thought.

Relaxing music, especially of the *New Age* genre, induces an atmosphere of relaxation and distraction thanks to its large number of instruments that imitate the sounds of nature.

6. Change habits

It is quite possible that the thoughts that worry us are linked to some action we perform every day, although it may seem that their appearance is completely random and for no apparent reason.

Working on the worry itself is quite complicated, but making a change in a person's habits is not so complicated.

That is why it can be very beneficial to make some small changes in your day-to-day life, such as going to new places, reconnecting with old friends... in essence, subjecting yourself to new stimuli.

If the change is made in a radical way, one must be careful, as it is not easy to introduce several new habits at the same time.

If achieved, it can be a great source of liberation since the new tends to occupy more prominence in mind than the old, which is where obsessive thoughts are found. In this way, we will pay more attention to new experiences.

7. Set a new goal

Closely related to the previous point, you can consider reaching a new goal, which will cause you to devote more attention to it than to invasive thoughts.

However, this strategy can be a double-edged sword. If done poorly, you run the risk of it becoming one of many projects you have started and failed to finish, in turn becoming an invasive thought.

That is why the new goal must be realistic but also challenging. An example of this type of project would be to start a collection, make a model or a puzzle, and obtain a B2 in English...

If the activity is truly pleasurable, you will devote attention to it not only while you are doing the activity, but also when you are not doing it, especially because you feel like doing it.

8. *Mindfulness*

This type of meditation technique has been one of the most studied in the field of psychology and that is why it is known to have many benefits in reducing anxiety and, at the same time, obsessive thoughts.

During the sessions in which this activity is carried out, you can concentrate on physical sensations, breath control, and the voice of the activity guide...

You enter a state of deep tranquility in which negative thoughts seem to dissipate more and more.

9. Physical exercise

It is well known that exercise is a good ally of both physical and mental health and it is a must when learning to stop thinking so much.

Not only does it have the great advantage of producing endorphins, but also, especially in directed activities, it allows you to focus on aspects such as posture and the correct execution of the movement.

In addition, once the exercise session is over, changes are initiated that are beneficial to the proper functioning of the body.

10. Walk

Related to the previous point, walking is also an effective ally to fight against the intrusion of unwanted thoughts.

While walking, we do not only move our legs, we also observe the places we pass by. Therefore, if you want to stop thinking about obsessions, it would be ideal to visit a bucolic place like a park or a mountain, where there are no distractions or the noise of the city.

The fresh air of the countryside has a relaxing effect on the organism, in addition to the fact that, by nature, human beings associate the green color of grass with calm and well-being.

As it is a different environment from what you are used to, especially if you are from the city, seeing wild flowers and plants also allows you to focus your attention on the trap that can become our mind.

CHAPTER 5

A life in balance: strategies, tips and final advice

Strategies to stop overthinking immediately

As we have already seen, thinking things through is important, but overanalyzing can lead to analysis paralysis.

In addition, if your mood is negative, overthinking things can lead you to find arguments to belittle what is undoubtedly extraordinary in your life.

If you are one of those people who think about every issue or problem, no matter how small it may be, or you analyze to satiety everything that happens, I am going to tell you 9 strategies to stop thinking too much immediately.

I guarantee that, if you put them into practice frequently, you will be able to reason in a more effective way without maximizing the consequences or being held back by your fears, and above all, you will achieve greater peace of mind and well-being in your life.

1. See things in perspective
It is very common to make a mountain out of a molehill. So when you are going over and over the same issue, think or write on a piece of paper: what importance will this have for me in 3 weeks? or 3 months? and in 3 years?

If the answer is none, what are you still doing thinking about it?

Ask yourself: is there anything more important that I really need to take care of?

Surely the answer is yes.

Therefore, when you get into a mental loop, ask yourself these simple questions: they will provide you with a broader view of your situation and that will allow you to direct your energy to those things that are really important in your life.

2. Set deadlines to make your decisions
If you don't put an expiration date on the decision you have to make, you are likely to look at it and analyze it from too many points of view.

Once you make a decision, you are completely free of the internal discourse that leads you to consider each of the options.

I'm sure you know someone who has wasted a year looking at homes before buying theirs and is ultimately unhappy with the decision.

Does it really make sense to prolong a decision too long?

I have it very clear: NO

I challenge you to reduce your decision-making timelines:
For small decisions such as: "Do I do yoga now or later?", "Do I buy the usual brand of turkey or this one that is on sale?", etc., don't take more than 30 seconds to make the decision.

For major decisions, I recommend giving yourself a reasonable amount of time, such as at the end of the day or at the end of the week. What you have to make is a firm commitment not to exceed that limit.

Think that once you make a decision, you will never know what would have happened if you had made a different choice. So, imagining the many different situations that would have occurred will not solve anything but rather rob you of your well-being and your ability to enjoy the present moment.

3. Take action

If you get used to taking immediate action, you will avoid procrastinating by overthinking. By committing to getting things done by a set deadline, you will become an action-oriented person.

I advise you to break down tasks into smaller ones, so that you can focus on achieving a small, more easily achievable goal.

This way, you will avoid feeling overwhelmed by the need to do something that is difficult to manage and that makes you fall into procrastination over and over again.

4. Internalize this: you can't control everything

If you think about things a hundred times, it may be because you have a certain addiction to wanting to control everything.

It may be because you have a terrible fear of failure, failure or making a fool of yourself.

But these things are inevitable in life, and even more so if you want to broaden your experience and grow by going beyond your comfort zone.

Think of people who are truly inspiring to you and look at their track record: you will see that they have also made mistakes, and many of them, to achieve their goals.

Mistakes can cause you to have a hard time when you make them, but if you look at them in a positive way, you will see that they are all important learning experiences.

Notice that worrying is a mental discourse process that happens before you can deal with something, but if it is out of your control, how can you deal with it?
Simplify that thinking this way:

Do you have a problem? Don't worry, stop overthinking and focus on the solution. And if you don't, accept it, be thankful for the learning and keep walking.

Therefore, stop trying to control everything: you simply cannot anticipate everything that may happen, nor do you have control of all the variables.

5. Divert your attention from situations that promote negative internal discourse.
Let's take an example: yesterday, I was hungry and was about to cook. I couldn't find the kitchen scissors and I needed them. My immediate mental reaction was to get angry and start arguing with myself mentally.

Then I realized it was silly to get angry about it and decided to use a knife instead. Maybe it could have been due to the bad mood that can arise when hungry.

The good thing is to identify it and when you are about to get angry, you can say out loud: "it's not worth it" or "I don't want to get angry" or simply "next!" and deal with the issue, instead of continuing to generate a maze in your head that seems endless.

This is a way for you to identify those situations in which your mood is inappropriate and you tend to engage in negative inner discourse, so that you can be alert and stop it in time to deal with the issue in a more appropriate mood.

You will find that, in most cases, the problem is very small or non-existent.

And if the problem is really important, then you will be in a better position to deal with it.

6. Don't drown yourself in uncertain thoughts

Another quite common habit, which often leads to endless internal speeches, is when there is fear about something completely uncertain.

In these cases, the most negative minds imagine all kinds of catastrophic scenarios, i.e., they put themselves in the worst-case scenario.

I have suffered terrible things in my life, although most of them never happened.
If you are one of these people, I suggest you ask yourself the following questions:
-   What is really the worst that can happen?
-   What is the real probability of that happening?

I have observed that when some uncertain fear comes to my mind and I respond realistically and honestly, most of the time, the answer is nothing/none or almost nothing/none.

When this type of uncertainty invades you, stop for a few minutes to ask yourself these questions: you will see reality in a clearer way, which will save you the energy that you would otherwise waste thinking about this uncertain fear.

7. Play sports

It may seem strange to you, but it helps me a lot. Sport has the extraordinary effect of releasing tensions and with them recurring negative thoughts.

The Greeks said it more than 5000 years ago, "Mens sāna in corpore sānō".

In short, it is more than proven that doing sports helps to have a clearer and freer mind.

8. Practice *mindfulness*

Mindfulness is a meditative technique based on mindfulness in the present moment.

When you are thinking about things from your past with worry, think that they are not going to change and that, therefore, the only thing you can do with them is to learn from what happened.

If the future is on your mind, it has not yet arrived and has a high degree of uncertainty. You cannot control the future and, therefore, you should not spend too much time planning.

The only thing you possess is the present and it is in that present that you must put your energy.

I will briefly tell you some tips:
- **Focus on the breath:** the breath is something that is always present and constantly accompanies us, which is why it is so effective and accessible when it comes to stop thinking too much. When something keeps bouncing around in your head, find your breath and focus on it.
- **Concentrate on noises:** closing your eyes and focusing your attention on the sounds around you is another exercise that will allow you to free your mind from thoughts.
- **Concentrate on the action:** for example, if you are washing the dishes, feel the touch of the dishes, the water, the temperature. In other words, focus your attention on what you are doing instead of what is going on in your head.

These are basic exercises that you can easily practice.

There are many other techniques, but I don't want to bore or saturate you with so many ideas. I encourage you to research the technique that most interests you and start practicing it on a regular basis. You will see positive changes sooner than you think.

9. Surround yourself with things that do not encourage you to think too much.

We are not alone in the universe and spend much of our time interacting with other people, so our relationships have an important influence on us.

And I'm not just talking about your groups of friends or family, but what you read in *blogs*, newspapers or what you see on TV. I decided some time ago not to listen to news channels because there was always news that made me indignant or produced bad energy in some way.

Therefore, I preferred to limit the information to what could really directly affect me or my family.

This applies to social relationships: if you have a friend with a tendency to think too much and negatively, consider whether he or she is good company.

I encourage you to spend more time with those people who positively affect your thinking and, therefore, your life.

Other strategies endorsed by experts to stop thinking too much

Is overthinking one of your biggest problems? If you are one of those who spend most of your time ruminating on thoughts, it's time you learned some expert-tested techniques to stop doing it. Overthinking not only keeps your head busy but also creates unnecessary stress, which can end up damaging your health in different ways.

Start by recognizing it

You can't accept that something is wrong and start to fix it, if you don't first identify what is going on.

If you find yourself in situations where your thoughts keep repeating over and over again and you end up stressed or feeling anxious, lacking energy, or with a headache; if you spend all day thinking about what a person said about a subject or even find yourself having imaginary conversations for more than 5 minutes and realize that you are doing nothing more than that, it would be important to recognize that you may be thinking too much. Try to identify those physical sensations or anxiety symptoms that appear from the stress of what you are experiencing. Also, try to find the root cause or reason why you are in this state of overthinking and try to minimize or eliminate the cause.

Observe and do not assume
Remember that these thoughts are not the facts. You must learn to discern and put distance between your identity and the thoughts that cloud your reality.

Ernest Rasyidi, M.D., a psychiatrist at St. Joseph Hospital, says, "Instead of emphasizing trying to stop worrying, the focus should be on doing positive things that you can control or manage.

Put time on your worries
Psychotherapist Natacha Duke of the Cleveland Clinic proposes the strategy of setting a daily time period for worrying.

That is, take some time out of your day (preferably between 10 to 30 minutes) to write down all your worries on a sheet of paper. Once you have made a list, visualize which of these worries have a solution and, above all, which ones are under your control.

Then, work on brainstorming to find solutions to those that are possible and, for those that are not, in your next period of concern, set aside a moment to accept them, let them go and free yourself.

Distracts the mind

Trick your brain and your thoughts. The worries may not go away and they may be real, but changing the routine with some activity you enjoy will allow you to stop thinking the same ideas over and over again.

In this case, experts suggest that you learn to develop a new skill that interests you: take a class or training that you haven't tried so far and would like to try, start a new hobby, do some service or volunteering (learning to play an instrument, for example, has many benefits).

Take a break

Expert Jeri Coast, director of clinical operations at Lightfully Behavioral Health, recommends that when you find yourself thinking about things over and over again, simply take a break to clear your head so you can see the context of the problem more clearly.

This will also allow you to recognize the emotions that arise behind negative thoughts and, in this way, you will create awareness so that you can change your mindset and thus begin to feel self-compassion for yourself and stop punishing yourself when you are not as perfect as you would like to be.

Get active

Dr. Matt Angelelli, a psychiatrist at Orlando Health in Florida, says exercise is the most important technique for treating anxiety and worry.

The practice of sports is a fundamental tool that enables physical and emotional well-being. When faced with situations in which it is difficult to stop thinking, it is recommended to do some physical activity to the person's liking because, among many other benefits, it produces the release of endorphins, the hormones linked to happiness.

In addition, exercise requires a person's concentration for proper execution. And it is a very positive thing that you can focus on the present while exercising instead of ruminating your thoughts over and over again.

Exercise does not have to be intense or performed for long hours to stop thinking too much. After just a few minutes, you will notice the beneficial effects on your mental balance and well-being.

Identifies success

If you are an expert at recognizing and digesting the bad over and over again, why not do it with the good?

Every time you catch yourself overthinking, take note and write down 5 things that went well throughout your week and also how you felt when they happened.

You don't need to win the lottery or receive recognition for being the best employee of the month. The mere fact that you can recognize the positive in even the smallest detail can be a great help and a very healthy and effective way to face or overcome many situations in your life.

Repeat the negative thought until it is assimilated

If you think too much, you are usually not aware of it until you are immersed in an unnecessary waste of time or you feel tired, dizzy or anxious.

Psychologist Julie Pike recommends summarizing the recurring thought in a conscious way in less than ten words over and over again. It may sound strange, but now you'll see why: for example, instead of repeatedly thinking: "I blew the job interview, I could have done better, I should have lied, others are better than me", etc... change all that to "I blew the interview".

Then, consciously think that phrase over and over again, even say it out loud. That will stop the brain from considering that thought as a threat. Why? Because the brain tends to identify each new thought as an independent threat. Since it is not something new and has been done consciously, the brain will look for the next automatic, unconscious task or thought.

Let go of perfectionism

Overthinking is associated with the idea that you could have done something or other better in order to avoid the unpleasant outcome.

Experts suggest avoiding perfectionism at all costs, assuming risks and fears, implementing new ideas or actions, making mistakes and moving forward even when situations are difficult. That's what living is all about and besides, it's part of human nature, isn't it?

Limits the use of media and social networks.
Much of what you worry about is not in your reality or in your present. An example of something that triggers these imaginary worries are the negative effects of the news, or the comparisons you can create in your mind about what is happening in the "perfect" world of social media.

You need to curb this type of consumerism and start being more aware of your use of social media and technology. It is important to focus from time to time on what is going on around you and, in this way, minimize or totally eliminate the harmful effect caused by all of the above.

Start working on self-compassion
What about your internal dialogue? You are either your best friend or your most feared enemy. Being accepting, loving, forgiving and kind to yourself can make a big difference between having a calm mind or being shipwrecked in the worst of storms.

Pay special attention to this.

Seek expert help or rely on therapy.
Overthinking is a bad habit and sometimes you won't be able to figure it out on your own.

Suppose you are immersed in a situation where you can't stop thinking. In that case, it is difficult to concentrate or do your daily activities and you notice that this interferes with your life, it is good to get support from an expert specialist in anxiety disorders or approach therapy groups such as cognitive behavioral therapy, so you can acquire tools and long-term strategies to help you deal with this.

Perform artistic activities

Art can be presented in multiple forms such as theater, music, painting or sculpture, among others.

Therefore, if you are unable to stop thinking, it is highly recommended that you engage in an artistic activity that you enjoy, as your energy will be redirected elsewhere. Consequently, the rhythm of your thoughts will be drastically reduced.

Breathing deeply

Elevated levels of tension are linked to muscular contractions that generate discomfort in the body. For this same reason, a person who is worried and does not stop thinking usually presents muscular difficulties.

In this way, inhaling and exhaling deeply continuously, as we have seen above, until you achieve greater relaxation is another very effective tool to stop thinking so much about situations that make you restless, stressful or anxious.

Understand that constant thoughts will not provide solutions.

Understanding that constant thinking will not bring about any kind of solution may be an alternative that allows you to give yourself a mental break from thinking so much about everything.

Eating a healthy diet

Certain foods contain properties that calm the central nervous system. A very good practice will be to follow a healthy diet based on green vegetables, fish, olive oil, fruits and legumes, taking into account that they can produce a fantastic relaxing effect on the body and, consequently, on your mind. To achieve this, it is necessary to consume healthy products every day.

There are also many relaxing herbs such as valerian, lemon balm, passionflower, chamomile or lavender, which can also help us to relax and stop thinking so much.

Read
Reading is a habit that can bring many benefits to people's lives. On the one hand, it fosters knowledge and on the other hand, reading requires mental concentration, so it is more possible for all other unnecessary thoughts to cease during reading.

How can I relax my mind?
While we cannot eradicate all stress from our lives, we can learn to manage it better. First, start by identifying and knowing your personal response to stress and also the type and number of stressors to which you are exposed.
What is it that keeps your mind on constant alert? What worries you most?

After identifying the problems, you can seek treatment. The possibilities are endless, from physical movement to nutrition, sleep, meditation and breathing. You can do a little of everything already discussed in this book to find out which technique you like best, or start with one of them and gradually incorporate others in a progressive and unhurried manner.

Here are four relaxation exercises that will help you relax your mind. They are suitable for beginners.

Learn to meditate

Once again: meditation will give you perspective. The Art of Living reports that meditating, much like deep breathing, will allow you to recognize your harmful and restrictive thought patterns. You will then be able to explore them further and in this way, you will be able to connect the dots and overcome your negative habits, such as finding fault with everything or pointing fingers or blaming people or situations.

The benefits of meditation are manifold and can be felt both physically and mentally. Many studies have shown that meditation has fantastic effects on stress relief, mental health, and even blood pressure control.

There are numerous ways to use meditation to reduce stress and anxiety, feel calmer and even address symptoms of depression. But remember, while meditation can be practiced in many ways, in essence, it all comes down to creating awareness and enhancing your mindfulness and focus on the present.

Visualization meditation is a great way to get started if you are new. Just like famous athletes practice visualizing their victory before they start to play to the best of their abilities, you can practice relaxing visualization meditation to relax or relieve anxiety.

Follow these steps to perform a basic visualization practice:
- Start by finding a quiet place to sit - on a cushion on the floor or in a chair.
- Set a timer for five to ten minutes.
- Keep your back straight. It may help to imagine that you have a rope running from the base of your spine to your back, neck and top of your head.

- Gently close your eyes.
- Imagine yourself in a quiet place: sitting on the grassy bank of a gently flowing river. The weather is perfect. The sun warms your skin and a cool, gentle breeze keeps you from getting too hot.
- You hear the water of the river running down. You feel the breeze on your skin. You smell the fresh scent of the flowers, the earth and the open air.
- Breathe slowly from your lower abdomen. Concentrate on the breath going in and out of your lungs. Try to inhale, filling your belly or abdomen first and then your lungs. You will empty your lungs first and then your belly as you exhale. Put one hand on your belly and one on your chest to notice how the air enters and where it settles.
- When a thought, feeling or emotion enters your mind, imagine that thought, feeling or emotion is sitting on a maple leaf floating in the river. See the leaf and what is on it. Accept that thought, feeling or emotion. It is not bad or good, scary, alarming, or worrisome. Simply look at it on the leaf and let it float away down the river. Return your focus to the breath and your visualization on the bank of the stream.
- Repeat the same process each time you experience a strange or automatic thought until the alarm clock goes off. Then, slowly release the image you have visualized. Before getting up, take a few minutes of silence before coming out of the meditative state.
- Achieving a meditative state will be a quick and easy process for you with regular practice. You will feel less physical tension in your body as you become more immersed in the practice.

Practice *mindfulness*

Mindfulness is another great practice for promoting peace and relaxation. It is quite similar to meditation, but it is different in the sense that you can practice mindfulness anytime, anywhere. The goal of mindfulness is to be present, simple as that.

Here's a basic *mindfulness* practice you can try while doing a chore-type activity, such as washing dishes at your kitchen sink:

- Stand in front of the sink. Focus on the fact that washing dishes will be the only thing you will be doing for at least the next ten minutes. Commit to this time.
- Before you start, you should tense as many muscles in your body as you can. Hold the tension for 3 seconds. Release. Rest for 5 seconds. Repeat this three times.
- How does your body feel right now? Notice if you are concentrating on a specific part of your body. Give your body a little shake to bring out any extra tension.
- Take three deep breaths, inhaling and exhaling. Any other thoughts knocking at the door of your mind? Tell them to go on their way.
- Turn on the faucet. Spend time getting the water temperature just right, not too hot and not too cold. Concentrate on the look and feel of the water as it glides through your fingers. Feel it go from cold to hot to warm. Listen as it runs out of the faucet and down the drain.
- Add a little soap to a sponge. Observe its bright color and notice its scent. Shake the sponge to create bubbles, watching the bubbles grow in number and feeling their warmth run across the skin of your hands. Feel every sensation your senses experience.

- Do you feel a strange thought or feeling come up? Observe it. Then let it pass. Return your attention to the soap and sponge.
- Take a plate to wash it. Examine the plate. Slowly begin to clean it, taking care to wash off every scrap of food.
- Rinse the dish, watching all the dirt stains and soapy water fall off. Set it aside to dry. Keep breathing deeply.
- Don't rush. Continue washing the dishes this way until you are done. Now, get a clean cup and pour yourself some herbal tea.

Practice yoga

Yoga is another excellent way to find peace and calm when you feel your mind is racing.

The mind-body connection with yoga is phenomenal. The theory behind the mind-body connection is that what happens in the mind (thoughts, emotions and feelings) affects what happens in your body, which in turn affects how you feel physically.

At the same time, how you feel physically and how healthy and fit your body is will affect your thoughts, feelings and emotions.

Yoga is a practice that takes into account the mind-body connection and aims to benefit all aspects of your being. Although, it may seem that the asanas (postures) only affect the physical aspect, your mental state is strongly influenced while practicing. Each posture can strengthen and improve the flexibility of the body while stimulating the organs and working on circulation. Each posture is also meant to stimulate the brain, inducing concentration and tranquility.

Try taking a yoga class or doing a lesson at home to take advantage of the many benefits of this practice. You'll leave the mat with less muscle tension, less stress and more focus.

Breathe better

Most of us take our breath for granted and underestimate the importance of breathing in our lives. We think that because our lungs work all the time without us having to tell them what to do, they must be doing the right thing and require no improvement. However, this is not entirely true. There are right and wrong ways to breathe.

Did you know that most people breathe too shallowly?

Many people breathe only the air that resides at the top of their lungs. This causes short, weak breaths that are tiring, and causes "stale" air to remain at the bottom of the lungs.

To check, place one hand on your stomach and the other on your chest. Breathe normally. Do you feel the hand on the belly rise as you inhale, or do you feel the hand on the chest rise? If you feel the hand on the chest rise first on the exhale, you are a shallow breather.

You should breathe from much lower down, taking in as much air as you can from the belly before it reaches your lungs. As you inhale, you should feel the hand on your belly rise first and when you have filled the capacity of your belly, the hand on your chest will also rise next.

Breathing exercises are often one of the most valuable techniques for calming the mind and helping to restore correct breathing patterns. Here's one to get you started:
   -   Find a quiet place to sit where your back is supported.

- Place one hand on the stomach and the other on the chest.
- Keep your back straight, pretending you have a rope running from the base of your spine up through your back and neck and out the top of your head.
- Slightly close your eyes.
- Take several deep breaths without thinking about how you are breathing.
- Now, take a deep breath and, as you inhale, feel your belly rise and your hand on your abdomen. Breathe slowly and, as you do so, say out loud: "I inhale tranquility and peace".
- When you can no longer take a breath, begin to slowly release your breath through your mouth. As you do so, you should say to yourself: "I exhale the tension and stress".
- Repeat this exercise for five to ten minutes or, if you are comfortable, for as long as you like.

Easy and simple relaxation tips!

Imagine you're about to go on stage for a big performance and your mind is racing. Try this mindful relaxation tip to regain some peace and tame racing thoughts.

- Find a quiet place: start by going to a quiet place to center yourself, the break room, dressing room, outdoors or even the bathroom.
- Sit down if possible: if you can, find a chair where you can sit with your back supported. Ideally, you should be able to rest your feet on the floor. Now, place one hand on your chest and the other on your stomach.

- Do a short breathing exercise: this exercise is called square breathing. You may also hear it called four-part breathing or 4x4 breathing. To do square breathing, follow the steps below:
    o Exhale all the air from your lungs.
    o Count to four slowly while inhaling through your nose only. As you inhale, you should feel the hand on your stomach rise. Your other hand should not move.
    o Slightly hold your breath for another four-second count.
    o Count to four one last time as you gently exhale the breath slowly through your mouth. The hand on your stomach should fall back down as you do this.
    o Repeat this exercise at least four times to relax and relieve stress.

How to calm my mind to sleep?

Sleep disorder is a common health problem that affects millions of people around the world. The truth is that anxiety and stress often come hand in hand with a lack of sleep. Whether poor sleep is caused by anxiety and stress or vice versa is a matter of debate and can be different from person to person.

However, one thing is for sure: calming your mind can significantly improve your sleep if you tend to have trouble falling asleep. To achieve a deeper state of sleep, try these mental relaxation tips:

Try a short meditation session before bedtime.
- Listen to white noise or nature sounds (such as waves or the murmur of a stream) while you fall asleep.

- Do 5 to 10 minutes of yoga at your bedside before going to sleep.
- Try practicing mindfulness while falling asleep (focusing on your breathing and the present moment and observing without interpreting your thoughts, feelings and emotions as they come and go).
- Listen to a recorded guided meditation before going to bed.
- Develop a nighttime routine in which you turn off all devices, dim the lights and put on your pajamas about a half hour before you intend to go to sleep.

Some thoughts and life lessons

"Close some doors today. Not because of pride, inability or arrogance, but simply because they take you nowhere." Paulo Coelho.

When we least expect it, life throws us a challenge to test our courage and willingness to change; at a time like this, it makes no sense to pretend that nothing has happened or to say that we are not ready. The challenge will not wait for our indecision. We can let it pass us by and learn something from it or face it and overcome it to grow a little more at different levels.

Don't give explanations. Your friends don't need them and your enemies won't believe them.

There is suffering in life, and there are defeats. No one can avoid them. But it is better to lose some of the battles in the fight for your dreams than to be defeated without knowing what you are fighting for.

Our true friends are those who are with us when good things happen. They cheer us on and take pleasure in our triumphs.

When someone leaves, it is because someone else is coming.

Some people seem to be happy but simply do not attach much importance to the matter. Others make plans: I'm going to have a husband, a home, two children, and a house in the country. While they are busy with that, they are like bulls looking for the bullfighter: they react instinctively, and they make mistakes, not knowing where the target is. They get their car, and sometimes they even get a Ferrari, they think that is the meaning of life and never question it. However, their eyes betray the sadness that not even they know they carry in their souls.

Close some doors today. Not out of pride, inability or arrogance but simply because they get you nowhere.

It is always important to know when something has come to an end. Closing circles, closing doors, ending chapters, no matter what we call it; what matters is to leave in the past those moments of life that have passed.

Love is always new. Regardless of whether we love once, twice or a dozen times in our lives, we are always faced with a completely new situation.

Love can send us to hell or to paradise, but it always takes us somewhere. We simply have to accept it because it is what nourishes our existence. If we reject it, we starve because we lack the courage to reach out and pluck the fruit from the branches of the tree of life. We have to take love to the very place where we find it, even if it means hours, days or weeks of disappointment and sadness. The moment we begin to look for love, love begins to look for us. And it is to save us.

It is said that the darkest hour of the night comes just before dawn.

Everyone believes that the main goal in life is to follow a plan. They never ask if that plan is theirs or if it was created by someone else. They accumulate experiences, memories, things, and ideas from other people, which is more than they can bear. And that's why they forget to fight for their own dreams.

Tragedy always provokes a radical change in our lives, a change that is associated with the same principle: loss. In the face of any personal loss, there is no point in trying to recover what has been; the best thing to do is to take advantage of the great space that opens up before us and fill it with something new.

I forgive for the tears they made me shed, I forgive the pain and disappointments, I forgive the betrayals and lies, I forgive the slander, I forgive the hatred and persecution, I forgive the blows that hurt me, I forgive the shattered dreams, I forgive dead hopes, I forgive hostility and jealousy, I forgive indifference and ill will, I forgive injustice committed in the name of justice, I forgive anger and cruelty, I forgive negligence and contempt, I forgive the world and all its evils.... I also forgive myself.

May the misfortunes of the past no longer weigh on my heart. Instead of pain and resentment, I choose understanding and compassion. Instead of rebellion, I choose the music of my violin. Instead of sorrow, I choose oblivion. Instead of revenge, I choose victory.

I will be able to love, regardless of whether I am loved back; I will be able to give, even when I have nothing; to work happily, even in the midst of difficulties; to reach out my hand, even when I am completely alone and abandoned; to dry my tears, even when I cry; to believe, even when no one believes in me.... So it is. So it shall be.

When I had nothing left to lose, they gave me everything.

When I stopped being who I am, I found myself. When I experienced humiliation and yet kept walking, I understood that I was free to choose my destiny.

Resetting the mind to achieve peace of mind, balance, well-being and ward off negative thoughts is something we should all set out to do but rarely do because we think 'that's just the way we are', an idea that mental health experts believe is totally wrong.

If we were aware of how we sabotage ourselves every day and that, perhaps, this mental 'crushing' is the cause of our discomfort, we would look for ways to reverse it. Moreover, even if it means an effort, it is possible to change our way of thinking little by little, although sometimes we need extra help.

The mind can be a wonderful place or, on the contrary, a hell. The positive thing is that, except if there is a pathology, which requires external help, it usually depends on ourselves and that, with a few simple exercises, we can 'reset' the mind and keep away the negative thoughts, the anticipations that cause us discomfort and uneasiness.

Juan Carlos Álvarez Campillo, author of the *best-seller* The Mental Trainer, psychologist and expert in leadership and *coaching* of top athletes and top executives in Spain, gives us, for example, five keys that can help us become an ally of our own mind, instead of its enemy. For example:
- Several times a day, stop for 10 seconds and be aware of what you are thinking about.
- Once you have identified the thought, observe if it is positive or negative, if it helps or hurts you and what emotion it produces: anger, sadness, joy, anxiety...
- If the thought is positive, treasure it, empower it. If the thought produces a negative emotion, distance yourself from it. You can say to yourself: that thought is not me, it does not represent me, it is something unconscious or a passing state of mind.
- Replace negative thoughts with others that are more enriching and that give you good feelings. For example, do something that you like, talk to someone who makes you feel good, enjoy a walk, a good meal...

- Reinforce all of the above by practicing relaxation therapies or techniques. For example, you can concentrate on breathing for about five minutes.

Silence therapy

Something as simple as spending some time in silence can quiet our minds.

"Silence is a natural and simple therapy. It is highly recommended for anyone, but especially for those with excessive stress and anxiety, whether or not they have nervous problems.

It is advisable a daily time of introspection, in silence, with our reflective thoughts. It will be tremendously positive to subtract these minutes from external demands, cell phones and the noise and distraction of social networks".

Group therapy

Group therapy can be a good ally in certain personal situations, in which you share similar experiences with other people and so the support and understanding of the group is therapeutic in itself.

For this, it is essential that the person appreciates and is grateful for these moments and benefits and feels comfortable in a group.

Another tool we have to reset our minds is to seek the help of a professional or *coach to* help us become aware of our areas of improvement, help us set goals and encourage us to achieve them. An adequate and brief counseling process can be very powerful and therapeutic.

CONCLUSION

The syndrome of accelerated thinking or the habit of thinking too much is something very common in today's world. We live in a world full of distractions and stimuli, noise, hurry and responsibilities, pressures and excesses. Overthinking is a consequence of all of the above. It is not your fault, it is not something you have done wrong. We have simply become accustomed to living this way and we have normalized it until a moment comes when our body gives us a warning in the form of a symptom: anxiety, insomnia, stress, depression. And then it is our responsibility to modify our habits or incorporate new ones to nip that negative trigger in the bud and prevent it from continuing to bear such bad-tasting fruit.

Allow your mind to slow down, turn off the lights or go on vacation for a few moments by practicing any of the many techniques I have shared with you. That way, little by little, you will be able to regain control of your mind and use it properly for your benefit, happiness and well-being.

By the way: the ONLY thing, or at least, the most powerful action that drives, creates or enhances our happiness, is GRATITUDE. Thank out loud every day for a few minutes for everything you feel is a fortune, blessing or privilege to have in your life, and believe me, you will be creating abundance, health, love and success in your life. "Thanks for another day on my feet", "thanks for the house I live in", "thanks that my parents are alive", "thanks for the partner that I have, that understands me, loves me and supports me", "thanks for my couple", "thank you for the abundance I have in my life", "thanks for the life I have". "Thanks for the earth", "thanks for my desire to improve", "thanks for the obstacles that make me grow more and more", "thanks for having food", "thanks for being alive", etc, etc, etc, etc....

What you focus on is what you attract, but not only that. Your attention is the lens through which you look at your life. If you see through gratitude, little by little, you will see more and more reasons to be grateful and that, without a doubt, will change your life for the better, and then you will have the wonderful power to feel more and think less.

Thank you for reading this book.

Have a safe trip!
Ryan Cross

BONUS

Bonus 1
Affirmations for self-transformation

Affirmations are positive statements that help you to reprogram your mind and foster positive change in our life. In the context of the Enneagram, we can use specific affirmations based on each personality type to promote self-transformation and personal growth.

Below, let's look at which affirmations are effective in helping each personality type on a day-to-day basis:

Type 1 - The Perfectionist Personality

I am enough just the way I am. I allow myself to make mistakes and learn from them.

I recognize that progress is more important than perfection. I allow myself to grow and evolve rather than seek absolute excellence.

I appreciate my accomplishments and recognize that success is not determined solely by the end results, but by the effort and dedication I put into each task.

Type 2 - The Helper

I value my own well-being and set healthy boundaries. I allow myself to be supported and cared for.

I learn to say "no" when necessary and set healthy boundaries to maintain my emotional and physical well-being. I recognize that taking care of myself enables me to be better able to help others more effectively and sustainably.

Type 3 - The Achiever Personality

My value is not dependent on my external accomplishments. My authenticity is my greatest strength.

My worth is not tied solely to my external accomplishments, but to my authenticity and the quality of my personal relationships.

I appreciate moments of rest and enjoyment, recognizing that true happiness does not depend solely on achieving goals, but on enjoying the journey.

Type 4 - The Individualist

I celebrate my uniqueness and accept myself in all my facets. My creativity lights my path.

I explore and embrace my inner diversity. Every part of me has its purpose and contributes to my uniqueness and personal growth.

I appreciate the power of my creativity and allow it to guide my choices, bringing new perspectives and opportunities into my life.

Type 5 - The Investigator

I trust my inner wisdom and share my knowledge with others. I am part of the whole.

I trust my intuition and inner wisdom when making decisions and seeking knowledge. My unique perspective enriches my environment and benefits others.

I generously share my knowledge and experiences, knowing that in doing so, I contribute to the growth and development of those around me.

Type 6 - The Loyalist

I trust myself and the process of life. I am courageous and able to face any challenge.

I trust myself and my ability to face challenges. I am constantly growing and developing and have the courage to overcome any obstacle that comes my way.

I cultivate relationships based on loyalty and mutual trust, creating a supportive and collaborative environment in my life.

Type 7 - The Enthusiast

I find fulfillment in the present and appreciate the blessings of each moment. Joy is within me.

I find joy and fulfillment in each present moment, appreciating the little things that bring me happiness and gratitude.

I cultivate a mindset of abundance and optimism, recognizing that joy and happiness are inner states that I can nurture and experience at any moment.

Type 8 - The Protector Personality

I am strong and powerful, allowing myself to be vulnerable and show compassion toward others.

I recognize my personal strength and power, and also allow myself to show vulnerability and compassion to others.

I use my strength and protection to care for and support those I care about, creating a safe and loving environment around me.

Type 9 - The Peacemaker Personality

I assert myself and express my needs clearly and assertively. My voice is important and valued.

I assert and express my needs and desires clearly and respectfully, knowing that my voice and opinions are important and valued.

I seek harmony and peaceful conflict resolution, creating a space where everyone feels heard and understood.

For good use of these and other positive affirmations, it is advisable to:

Be aware of your thoughts: Observe your thoughts and detect negative or limiting patterns. Identify the beliefs you want to change and replace them with positive affirmations.

Choose powerful affirmations: Create affirmations that resonate with you and are relevant to your personal growth. They should be positive, in the present tense and in the first person.

Repeat and reinforce: Repeat your affirmations daily, preferably in moments of peace, when waking up or before going to sleep. Reinforce their effectiveness by visualizing yourself living the reality you desire while reciting them.

Reinforce your affirmations with consistent actions: Affirmations are most effective when they are accompanied by consistent actions. Align your actions and behaviors with the beliefs and attitudes you wish to manifest in your life.

By using affirmations based on each Enneagram personality type, you can direct your focus to the specific aspects you wish to strengthen and transform in your life.

Remember that affirmations are not a magic bullet, but a tool to help you reprogram your mind and create positive change in your life.

Using effective affirmations requires commitment and consistent practice. As you practice and commit to affirmations, you will gradually begin to cultivate a more positive, confident and empowered mindset.

Change takes time and effort. Be patient with yourself and maintain an attitude of openness and receptivity. Don't expect instant results, but practice consistently and trust the process. By adopting positive and realistic affirmations, you can reprogram your mind and begin to align your thoughts, beliefs and actions with your true potential.

Don't be discouraged if at first you don't feel an immediate change, consistent practice and perseverance are key to lasting results. Over time, affirmations can help you change your negative thought patterns, strengthen your self-confidence and enable you to achieve your goals and aspirations.

Tailor affirmations to your own language and way of thinking. Choose words and phrases that create a sense of connection and empowerment, affirmations should be realistic and believable to you, as your mind needs to accept them as true for them to be effective.

As you practice affirmations consistently and integrate them into your daily life, you will begin to notice positive changes in the way you think, feel and act. For example, if you affirm that you are a healthy person, support that affirmation with healthy food choices and regular exercise.

Powerful affirmations can be an invaluable tool for self-transformation and personal growth. By combining effective affirmations with clear visualizations and consistent actions, you can cultivate a positive mindset and build a life more aligned with your true self.

Bonus 2
Cultivating Emotional Resilience

Emotional resilience is an essential skill for facing life's challenges and adversities with strength and adaptability. It allows us to bounce back from difficulties and maintain a positive attitude.

Emotional resilience is essential to our emotional and mental well-being, helping us to cope with stressful situations, overcome failures and maintain a positive mindset. By cultivating it, we develop the ability to manage our emotions in a healthy way and build a solid foundation for personal growth.

There are several aspects of our personality that emotional resilience can strengthen. For example:

Adaptation to change: it allows us to adapt to life's changes and transitions more effectively. It helps us to accept and overcome obstacles, finding new opportunities in the midst of adversity.

Stress management: Helps us to manage stress more efficiently. It allows us to identify our emotional responses to stressful situations and take measures to reduce the negative impact of stress on our health and well-being.

Self-confidence: Strengthens our self-confidence. It helps us believe in our abilities to overcome challenges and gives us the courage to face difficult situations.

There are several practices that can help you strengthen your emotional resilience. Here are some recommended exercises and techniques:

Emotional self-awareness: take time to explore and understand your own emotions. Practice mindfulness and introspection to recognize your emotional patterns and how they affect you. This will allow you to develop a greater awareness of yourself and your emotional responses. Building a support network: Cultivate strong, supportive relationships with family, friends and members of your community. Share your feelings and experiences with people you trust, as this can provide you with the emotional support you need during difficult times.

Seek social support: Seek support from people close to you, such as friends, family or support groups. Sharing your experiences and emotions with others can help you gain different perspectives and feel understood. Participate in social activities that provide positive connections and allow you to feel part of a community.

Practice self-compassion: Learn to treat yourself with kindness and understanding when you face challenges or make mistakes. Recognize that we all make mistakes and that personal growth involves learning from them. Instead of judging yourself harshly, practice self-compassion and give yourself permission to be human.

Maintain a learning attitude: Cultivate a mindset that is open and receptive to continuous learning. Consider every experience as an opportunity to grow and learn more about yourself. Be curious and willing to explore new perspectives and approaches to life.

Acceptance and adaptation: Learn to accept circumstances that you cannot change and focus on adapting to them. Recognize that change is an inevitable part of life and look for new ways to approach challenges.

Practice problem solving: Develop effective problem solving skills. Break challenges into smaller, more manageable steps and look for creative solutions. This will help you face obstacles with a proactive mindset.

Self-care: Prioritize your physical and mental well-being. Spending time on activities that bring you joy, rest and rejuvenation is critical to cultivating emotional resilience. Set healthy boundaries in your life and learn to say "no" when necessary. Self-care also involves maintaining a balanced diet, getting enough rest and maintaining a proper sleep routine. Develop coping skills: Learn healthy coping techniques to manage stress and negative emotions. This may include regular physical exercise, relaxation techniques such as meditation or deep breathing, and pursuing activities that help you express your emotions, such as writing in a journal or practicing a hobby.

Cultivating positive thoughts: Practice gratitude and focusing on positive aspects of your life. Challenge your negative thoughts and replace them with positive affirmations. Make a list of past accomplishments and personal strengths to remind yourself of your ability to overcome obstacles and face challenges.

Developing emotional resilience is an ongoing process that requires practice and dedication. By strengthening our ability to manage emotions and adapt to difficult situations, we can face life's challenges with confidence and maintain a positive outlook.

Use these exercises and techniques to build a solid foundation for your emotional well-being and personal growth.

Remember to be kind to yourself during this journey of self-transformation.

Bonus 3
Building Healthy Relationships

Healthy and meaningful relationships are fundamental to our emotional and personal well-being. They provide us with support, companionship and a sense of deep connection. However, building healthy relationships can be challenging, as each individual brings unique experiences and patterns of behavior.

The foundation of any healthy relationship is open and honest communication, this involves:

Learning to express our feelings, thoughts and needs clearly and respectfully.

- Actively listening to your partner, friend or family member, showing genuine interest and empathy. Setting clear boundaries in relationships, this is essential to ensure mutual respect and emotional balance.
- Learning to say "no" when necessary and to set boundaries in uncomfortable situations.
- Trust is a fundamental pillar in healthy relationships. To build it, it is important to:
- Being authentic.
- Follow through on promises and commitments. Avoid manipulation, dishonesty and deception.
- Practicing empathy and understanding by putting yourself in the other person's shoes and validating their emotions and perspectives.
- Identifying and addressing toxic patterns, abusive behaviors or disrespect in relationships.
- Overcoming toxic patterns requires personal work and mutual commitment. You can seek professional support or consider therapy to work on healing and change.

It is important to remember that each relationship is unique and requires constant attention. By developing greater awareness of yourself and your relationship patterns, you will be able to nurture and strengthen your connections with others.

Remember that healthy relationships also involve taking care of yourself. Set boundaries and make time for physical and mental self-care.

By building healthy relationships, you will be cultivating an environment of support, trust and mutual growth. Through mindfulness and commitment, you can create lasting, meaningful relationships that propel you toward a fuller, more satisfying life.

Bonus 4

Visualization and personal transformation

Visualization can be an effective way to explore and deepen your inner self. It is a powerful tool that allows us to access our imagination and create vivid and meaningful mental images.

Through visualization, we can connect with our deepest goals, dreams and desires and use this powerful tool to enhance our self-awareness and personal growth.

In this bonus, we will learn some visualization exercises that will help us transform our lives in a positive and meaningful way.

Let's look at some visualization exercises that can help us boost our self-knowledge:

The Hall of Mirrors: Imagine you walk into a room full of mirrors. Each one reflects a different facet of your personality, your strengths, your weaknesses, your dreams and your fears. Look closely at each reflection and reflect on what it reveals about you. Use this visualization to gain a deeper understanding of who you are.

The Inner Garden: Close your eyes and imagine that you are walking through a beautiful garden. Each element of the garden represents an aspect of your life: the flowers symbolize your relationships, the trees represent your personal growth, the water reflects your inner tranquility. Notice how each element looks and how they interact with each other. Reflect on what you would like to change, improve or cultivate in your inner garden. Use this visualization to explore your desires and goals in different areas of your life.

Our imagination has a powerful impact on our perception and our ability to create positive changes in our lives. Let's use imagination as a tool for positive change.

Journey into the future: Close your eyes and imagine that you are in a distant future, where you have achieved all your goals and feel fully realized. Observe your life in this future and visualize all the details: how you feel, what you have achieved, how you relate to others, etc. Use this visualization to connect with your vision of success and to set clear and motivating goals in the present.

Transformation of limiting beliefs: Identify a belief that is holding you back from moving toward your goals. Close your eyes and imagine holding that belief in your hands. Visualize transforming that belief into something positive and empowering. Imagine the belief becoming a seed that you plant in the fertile soil of your mind, and enjoy how it grows into a new belief that strengthens you and propels you toward success.

Remember that visualization is a personal practice unique to each person. You can adapt the visualization exercises to your own needs and preferences. Find a quiet place, close your eyes, breathe deeply and immerse yourself in the imaginative experience.

By using these powerful visualizations, you will develop a deeper connection with yourself, discovering new possibilities and potential in your life.

Visualization not only helps you focus on your goals and dreams, but also provides you with an effective tool for overcoming obstacles, strengthening your confidence and awakening your creativity.

As you immerse yourself in your imagination, you open yourself to new perspectives and possibilities, creating a solid foundation for growth and positive change in your life. In this way, you can move toward manifesting your true self and living a full and meaningful life.

Visualizations are a valuable tool for personal transformation, allowing you to enhance your self-knowledge, explore your desires and goals, and transform limiting beliefs into empowering ones

BIBLIOGRAPHY AND SOURCES

- https://www.bbc.com/mundo/noticias
- Morin, A (2021). *How to Know When You're Overthinking.* Very Well Mind. https://www.verywellmind.com/how-to-know-when-youre-overthinking-5077069
- Hanson, R (2020). *Are You Thinking Too Much?* Psychology Today. https://www.psychologytoday.com/intl/blog/your-wise-brain/201711/are-you-thinking-too-much
- American Psychiatric Association (2014). *Diagnostic and Statistical Manual of Mental Disorders (DSM-5).* Madrid: Editorial Médica Panamericana.
- Abramowitz J. S., Schwartz S. A., Moore K. M., Luenzmann K. R. (2003). *Obsessive-compulsive symptoms in pregnancy and the puerperium: a review of the literature. J Anxiety Disord 17* (4): 461-78.
- Julien D., O'Connor K. P., Aardema F. (2007). "Intrusive thoughts, obsessions, and appraisals in obsessive-compulsive disorder: a critical review". Clin Psychol Rev 27 (3): 366-83.
- Payás Puigarnau, A. (2008). *Psychological functions and treatment of obsessive ruminations in bereavement.* Revista de la Asociación Española de Neuropsiquiatría, 28 (102), 307-323.
- https://www.ncbi.nlm.nih.gov/pmc/articles/PMC4526594/#__ffn_sectitle

- https://www.health.harvard.edu/blog/mindfulness-meditation-helps-fight-insomnia-improves-sleep-201502187726

Thank you for choosing my book!

I sincerely hope that you have enjoyed the journey through the pages of this book and that my experiences can help and motivate you to walk your own path towards personal growth, mental health and happiness.

Will you help me help others?

The best way to show me your support is thanks to a positive review or rating of my book on the page where you got it. It will take you a few seconds to do it, but it will mean a lot to me.

A good rating from you helps my work reach more people and positively impact their lives, health and well-being.

Thanks for everything, happy journey.
Ryan Cross

www.ingramcontent.com/pod-product-compliance
Lightning Source LLC
Chambersburg PA
CBHW050220270326
41914CB00003BA/495

9781960395375